CRITICAL THINKING

FOR EVERY CLASSROOM

M. Neil Browne

Chelsea Kulhanek

TABLE OF CONTENTS

Introduction for Teachers 4

Chapter One: Scams, Cults, Advertisements, Misinformation, Disinformation, and Well-Intentioned but Sloppy Thinking 9

Chapter Two: The Foundational Importance of the Questions "Why?" And "When?" 23

Chapter Three: The Relevance of Missing Information 28

Chapter Four: Misused Information 51

Appendix One: Summary 71

Appendix Two: Intellectual Benefactors 72

INTRODUCTION FOR TEACHERS

Teachers want what is best for their students. They choose a profession that promises to contribute to the creativity, knowledge, and emotional strength of tomorrow's innovators and servant-leaders. Teachers are fundamentally givers and only collaterally do they receive the joy of a front row seat to the lifelong impacts of their work.

The broader community expects them to nurture students. But paradoxically, governance controlling educators' compensation signals that teachers should serve important social needs while their salaries send a different message. Consequently, our educators have only limited status in a culture that frequently equates the worth of a person's life in dollars earned.

A 2022 study published in *Education Week*, featuring data compiled by scholars at Brown University, revealed a dramatic decline in teachers' job satisfaction overall. It is at its lowest level in 50 years, with 42 percent of educators saying the stress of their job is worth it, compared to 81 percent of educators in the 1970s. Moreover, interest in the teaching profession among high school seniors and college freshman is at its lowest in 50 years, dropping 50 percent since the 1990s, and 38 percent since 2010.[1]

Teachers find themselves struggling to convince a skeptical public that their work is essential to a healthy democracy and society. That work is multifaceted. But if there is a single educational goal proclaimed by educators at all levels, it would likely be critical thinking. If we lived in a world where truth and nonsense wore

---

[1] https://www.edweek.org/teaching-learning/teacher-job-satisfaction-hits-an-all-time-low/2022/04

clearly identifiable hats, we would not need to learn how to ask questions to distinguish between sense and nonsense. In such a world, we could trust that social media is not rife with conspiracy theories, disinformation, and misinformation. There would be little need to protect ourselves from advertisements that range from worthless to dangerous, questionable techniques to amass piles of wealth, diets or drugs with furtive side effects, or other far-fetched paths to certainty.

But we live in a different world, where mental hygiene (in the form of critical thinking) must be taught and learned. The attitudes and skills of critical thinking are neither part of our DNA nor sought-after by most humans. None of us can be expected to yearn for skills that we do not know we lack. Today, as ever, the cognitive health of a culture depends heavily on well-meaning teachers who model and share these attitudes and skills with their students.

Teachers at all levels of our educational system would love to enhance their students' critical thinking. However, their training and the expectations of the institutions where they teach present a troublesome paradox. Expressions of affection for critical thinking exist side-by-side with the widespread neglect of coursework focused on critical thinking.

Schools at all levels, teachers and business leaders swear their loyalty to practicing "critical thinking." However, except for a few courses in philosophy, statistics training, and the scientific method in science courses, the visible curriculum contains no explicit training in critical thinking. There are no departments of critical thinking with responsibility to champion critical thinking.

The critical thinking that is learned and then taught is usually linked to some of the more common problem areas in the discipline of our training. Psychologists are taught to ask questions related to the quality of our perceptions. Philosophers learn logic. Communication professionals learn about "our second language" --- the many body, facial, and tonal dimensions with which we try to express ourselves. Cognitive scientists study mental habits that create dangerous biases in our thinking.

But that silo mentality reduces curiosity about a full-throated critical thinking, one that applies the many forms of critical thinking whenever humans seek answers. No one is at fault here.

For most of us, our training has rigid boundaries, and it focuses on a specific set of questions, necessarily creating blind spots when questions require multi-disciplinary exploration.

How can such a universal goal be assigned so little space in our educational system? The best response we can muster is a phrase often used in analyses of failures of the human community to address environmental decay: *everyone's business often becomes no one's business*. In other words, because the environment is so fragile and universally significant to our way of living, there is no need for *me* to be paying attention to its problems, for *you* will surely be on duty guarding its integrity.

Analogously, individual classrooms need not focus on critical thinking because every classroom will naturally give it sufficient attention. This method of avoiding responsibility has been repeatedly documented when investigating why few rush to assist others in an emergency. We see many potential intervenors in the area and no need to push ourselves forward in a display of empathy.

To be a teacher is to have multiple pressures and responsibilities. Peer reviews, students with different learning capabilities, research expectations in our most acclaimed universities, grading responsibilities, and loyalty to our individual specialties leave little room for anything other than a laser focus on the specific curriculum of existing specialties. In short, teachers are busy, and they have little remaining time to teach anything else.

We have spent more than five decades trying to figure out why there is such a gap between the verbal devotion educators have for critical thinking and the disappointing mental performance of so many people who graduate from our schools. We talk about "thinking below the surface" and "doing deep dives" as we construct the thoughts and behaviors that shape our identities. But those signals about who we are become wise only after we have learned to ask questions that reveal the quality of the pathways we have travelled to form our beliefs, conclusions, and decisions ("BCDs"). In short, we need to learn and apply critical thinking.

This book is not a comprehensive critical thinking text. It is a book about *the essentials* of critical thinking.

Many of us look at the well-toned bodies of a yoga or Pilates guru as aspirational. But realistically, we do not have the time to imitate the hours and hours of exercise to mimic their physical conditioning. Instead, to maximize our own performance, we need coaching that does a couple of things: First, we need to know the exercises with the greatest impact to our sustained physical health. Second, we need to know where to find exercises to address our particular aches, pains, and goals.

When we decided to be teachers, we were motivated by empathy for learners rather than visions of mansions or the latest high-end Porsche. Our past teachers liberated us from layers of over-simplifications, blindness toward the rich tapestry of human imagination, and the flood of mistakes flowing from superficial knowledge. We cringe to think what our lives would have been like had our teachers not made our mental and emotional needs their focus.

Our book is simple enough that teachers need to spend very little time teaching critical thinking beyond providing advice and support for those who read the book. Critical thinking has dozens of components. When we organized this book, our emphasis was on clarity, including only the most powerful elements of critical thinking, and including illustrations of the skills. We recommend that, when allocating class time to this book, utilize and emphasis the critical thinking skills and material directly applicable to the subject matter in that class.

Our goal is efficiency, minimizing the need to formally teach dozens of critical thinking skills, while obtaining as much critical thinking training as possible. We are asking you to trust that we have included only the most valuable critical thinking skills that can protect the reader from the many skilled persuaders seeking their money, votes, time, and loyalty in this book. In addition, these skills provide a justifiable confidence that a critical thinker has chosen beliefs, conclusions, and decisions based on relevance, curiosity, respect for reason, informed choice of expertise, careful reliance on evidence, and humility.

CHAPTER ONE

SCAMS, CULTS, ADVERTISEMENTS, MISINFORMATION, DISINFORMATION AND WELL-INTENTIONED BUT SLOPPY THINKING

Humans have many brilliant moments of creativity and insight. Science has saved millions of lives and produced new technology that enriches nearly every modern moment. We should never allow the criticism of weaknesses in our thinking to make us overlook what human thinking and feeling has produced. It would be an outrageous mistake to see critical thinking as anything other than exploratory, tolerant, and beautiful. Humans created *King Lear,* impressionist music and art, the wheel, the airplane, libraries, the theory of relativity, Darwinism, and the tallest outside elevator in the world (1,070 feet down a sheer cliff in Zhangjiajie, China). And never forget the accomplishments represented in Exhibit 1-1.

Exhibit 1-1

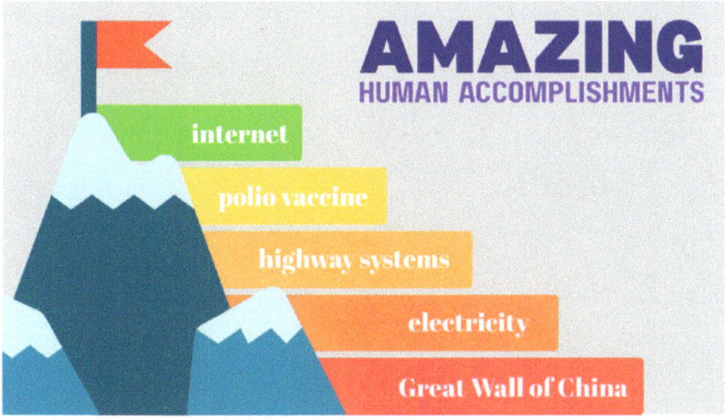

AMAZING HUMAN ACCOMPLISHMENTS

- internet
- polio vaccine
- highway systems
- electricity
- Great Wall of China

Critical thinking is an attempt to reduce the noise in human conversation and replace it with signals that highlight other achievements at the personal and community level. Even with humanity's success, we still harbor mental habits and other systematic flaws in thinking which cause us a slew of problems and take us down blind alleys.

Though quite painful to acknowledge, we make many mistakes. While researchers have defined "mistakes" in a diverse manner to form estimates, the published measurements say we make anywhere from 60 to 500 daily. We will let you imagine the extent of these blunders for periodic bouts with the discomfort of our imperfection.

Consequently, our minds need improvement. Critical thinking can sharply reduce our tendency to heed severely flawed reasoning by those who wish to control our beliefs, conclusions, and decisions (conveyed hereafter via the important acronym "BCD(s)"). Our money, loyalty, and time are precious resources valued by political ideologies, corporations, religions, thousands of internet trolls, and even those who love us. Critical thinking is a series of skills that serve as a shield against unreliable knowledge claims and evidence. Applying these skills will lead you to more reliable BCDs.

Visualize critical thinking as a set of filters. These filters give you a sense of having seized more control over your identity, who you are and who you will become. You are liberating yourself from those trying to persuade you with half-baked knowledge claims.

Other people want you to believe them. Typically, they are after your headspace because they: (1) want your money while giving you nothing or little in return, (2) desire your support to advance a vision they have of a better world, or (3) love you and believe they know better about what you need than you do. You may feel pressure to modify your views from every direction, as illustrated by Exhibit 1-2.

Exhibit 1-2

That third reason for wishing to persuade you is quite different from the first two reasons because these latter persuaders are on your side. They do not have some secret, behind-the-scenes rationale that benefits them at your expense. You owe it to them, the individuals who wish to persuade you toward well-being, to listen intently to their reasoning, in particular. They may know something you need to know. However, as a critical thinker, you would embrace what they wish you to accept not because of who they are or their intent, but because their thinking is evidence-based, ethical, and logical.

We must now be more precise about what "critical thinking" means in this book. The concept has many definitions. Yet the one central element of those varying definitions is the need to evaluate what we hear. As this chapter says over and over, in multiple ways, **persuasion moves you in its direction via a pathway created**

by others to bring you toward their BCDs. We call that pathway "reasoning." The combination of that reasoning with a belief, conclusion, or decision is called an "argument."

Note that this meaning of "argument" in critical thinking is about exploration and discovery; there is nothing hostile about it. The idea of "argument" represented in Exhibit 1-3 is altogether different from effective, growth-oriented critical thinking.

Exhibit 1-3

For our purposes, an example of an argument would be, "My optometrist warned me about those light bulbs. Therefore, I refuse to visit people who insist on using those bulbs." Together, those two sentences form an argument. Critical thinking focuses on the first sentence, "My optometrist warned me..." because its purported reliability shapes the quality of the second sentence.

Critical thinking is NOT a criticism of a BCD. Instead, it is the careful study of the *quality of the reasoning* being offered on behalf of a BCD. Critical thinking weighs the quality of the reasoning by using the filters we mentioned earlier to make a judgment about quality. For example, suppose one of us insisted that, in the seas surrounding Australia, the Giant Pacific Octopus will sometimes tuck itself into the nearest Giant Clam to protect itself from dangers of the Great Barrier Reef.

Our initial reaction to this, or any BCD, should be both curiosity and receptivity. But we would be more likely to accept a BCD if a marine biologist showed us pictures of an octopus peeking out from the mouth of a monstrous bivalve than if we had said something like "I saw it on the internet." In this instance, the REASON for believing is crucial, and should be our focus any time someone tries to persuade us of anything.

If you are starting to get into the spirit of this book, you might realize that you would like to ask the biologist some questions too. Do other clams serve as an octopus security system? Was the octopus in the photo dead or alive? Does the person who took the photo have skill with Photoshop or the assistance of AI? Is there observational data illustrating that the clam is not using the octopus for that clam's own protection against its predators? If questions like these reveal answers inconsistent with the conclusion of the person who started this conversation, we gain confidence that they are wrong.

The purpose of the rest of this chapter is to convince you that the quality of our lives requires persistent diligence in evaluating the many efforts to convince us to act, think, or believe in a certain manner.

SCAMS

A scam is a method of getting someone to give the scammer something while giving the person being scammed only a sense of anger mixed with the shame of being played for a fool. A con or scam artist knows how to take your money, giving you nothing in return but a horrible headache. They play on our emotions, promising huge payoffs for small investments. They may pose as representatives of agencies or professions you know and trust.

For instance, consider our grandparents, who were simple farmers, seemingly oblivious to scams. One afternoon, the night after a cyclone had cruised dangerously close to their farmhouse, four well-dressed men paid our grandparents a visit. When the men arrived, they asked whether they could check whether the cyclone had damaged my grandparents' home.

They looked around outside before asking to enter the home to explain their findings. But before they had started their report, the men eyed a book of hymnals on the piano.

Then the scam began. They asked whether my grandparents would say a prayer with them. The prayer asked for guidance in the decisions facing those whose property was damaged the fierce winds. Next, the leader of the quartet asked whether my grandparents would join them in a series of hymns. After 45 minutes of joyous singing, the sales pitch was brief and effective. My grandparents ended $16,000 poorer, having paid to repair a roof without a single loose shingle.

When we learn of a scam, nearly all of us wonder how anyone could be so incompetent as to fall for such an obvious fraud. We know with certitude that *we* would never be manipulated in that fashion. However, we are underestimating the ability of a colorful story told by a skilled, charismatic salesperson to reduce the skepticism we would ordinarily have.

For example, in 2003, Elizabeth Holmes was able to attract staggering investments for her fraudulent blood testing start-up from venerated businessmen including a Wal-Mart founder, the former head of the Council of Economic Advisors, the founder of Fox News, a former Secretary of Education, and a two-time U.S. Secretary of State.[2] More broadly, approximately 500,000 people are scammed every year.

---

[2] https://www.forbes.com/sites/petercohan/2016/12/01/how-theranoss-big-investors-were-taken/

Critical thinking can protect you from scammers.

CULTS

A cult is a group of people with excessive devotion to a person or belief system whose statements are the source of truth. Those who disagree with the cult leader are called "liars." Criticisms of the leader are called "persecution" and "fake news." The key to understanding cult members is realizing their acceptance of the leader's authoritarianism. They do not object to the leader's zero tolerance for criticism or the secretive financial affairs of the group.

Most cults fall into one of four categories:

1. Religious cults base their identity on spiritual dogma defined by the charismatic leader. Unlike most organized religions, cults are organized, operated and governed solely by the charismatic leader. As with scams, those who later abandon the cult are amazed at, and often confused by, how they tolerated the cult.

2. Sex cults tend to encourage unusual amounts of erotic activity among members, even including sexual abuse in some instances.

3. Political cults form when aligned ideological extremists transform from a political action organization in a democratic structure into an authoritarian framework. These cults often focus on hatred of groups seen as replacing the cult members' political and economic strength, *e.g.*, migrants. In this scenario, the cult leader promises revenge against those who have displaced the previously dominant group to its members.

4. "End of Days" or "doomsday" cults develop in anticipation of and preparation for the end of the world. When the prophesized end does not occur on the expected date, most cult members remain in the cult, supporting their leader's claims of new and improved projections for the end of time.

All cults share certain characteristics --- a charismatic leader with no accountability and physical and/or psychological abuse of members.

Because some see religions as cults, estimates of the number of cults and their members are difficult and range widely. The number of cults is likely something between 2,000 and 10,000; the number of Americans in cults ranges anywhere from 300,000 to three million. The point for us here is that many cults are open for business, and we are all the intended customers. Cults cleverly take advantage of those who are searching for community as a substitute for their loneliness.

ADVERTISEMENTS

Certain advertisements are valuable parts of a market economy. An ad that says, "Grass-fed hamburger tomorrow at Food Giant, $2.19 per pound," gives potential buyers information that would be extremely difficult for them to determine using their own knowledge base. The business provides a useful service when announcing what consumers would like to know for the benefit of the customer.

However, persuasive ads are those that are more than an announcement that a good or service is available. Persuasive advertising is the bulk of the advertising we experience. It is an effort to teach consumers that they need to buy what is being pitched based on an emotional appeal. The seller seeks control of your buying habits.

For example, imagine that a potato chip company advertises that we consumers should eat more of their potato chips because their potato chips are "lighter." The company made this claim because someone at their firm pointed out that many consumers are trying to reduce the fat in what they eat. However, when the state legislature in New York holds hearings asking executives for evidence that their chips have reduced fat, the executives look at each other in confusion and say, "Well, we do not have any such evidence." A legislator then says, "Then why did you make that claim?" What then, if the company's response is, "Just look at the color of our chips, they are much lighter in color than competing chips..."?

Advertisers are keenly aware of the frequent sloppiness of human decision making. Humorous advertising focused on lovable pets, families, popular sports figures, or children elicit in consumers an urge to buy whatever good or service is associated with the advertisement, even when there is no logical attachment between the advertising itself and the good or service being sold.

Lebron James is a phenomenal basketball player who has earned $900 million pitching products like Pepsi, Nike, and Beats by Dr. Dre. Yet as far as we know, he has no expertise at all in soft drink quality or consumption, footwear engineering, or the development of electronics.

While advertisers sometimes experience failed advertising campaigns, they usually sell products successfully. In other words, firms can rarely afford to hire influencers for hundreds of millions of dollars unless their experience says consumers will associate skill in one area (their company's field) with unusual skill in unrelated areas (that of the party doing the endorsing). Successful advertising, as Seth Godin points out in his book *All Marketers Are Liars*, is more often based on the story attached to the good or service than the characteristics of what is being sold. Again, advertisers realize the extent to which our thinking is flawed.

Similarly, political advertising is more about telling an attractive story than highlighting a candidate's policy proposals. An outstanding illustration is a successful effort by one political party to brand the Presidential candidate of the other Party as a war monger. A candidate for President once said that "Extremism in defense of liberty is no vice!"

The sixty-second advertising response of the other party features a young girl plucking the petals of a daisy one by one, making cute mistakes as she counts. Suddenly, a close-up of the girl's eye becomes a countdown for a nuclear explosion. The mushroom cloud expands as it begins its march of death. The implication was clear: "Vote for our candidate or risk destruction of the species."

To what extent do the manipulations in advertisements cause us to spend time and money in ways differing from a rational voter or buyer? Perhaps the start of answering that question is recognition that those who create the stories for these advertisements are making a huge bet that spending significant money pays a substantial return.

In other words, the cost of advertising returns profits that would not occur were voters and consumers more alert to the missing and false information permitting their advertising to flourish. The staggering success of advertisers in both the political sphere and private sector is measured by their ever-expanding budgets.

Is advertising a major assault on our choices? It is, immensely. Private sector advertising is expected to exceed $400 billion in 2024. US political ad spending will jump past $12 billion in 2024 --- a new high --- nearly tripling the $4.25 billion spent in 2016. Some of the top creative talents in our culture are united in persuading you to vote in a particular way. To claim that those with such staggering budgets do not know how to shift our choices significantly is wishful thinking.

MISINFORMATION AND DISINFORMATION

Misinformation refers to false factual claims that spread and infect our thinking <u>unintentionally</u>. For example, 42 percent of Americans claimed in President had caused massive unemployment in 2024. The fact, however, was the direct opposite. During his presidency, the country saw the longest duration of unemployment below four percent since the 1960s. Notably, when that President took office, the unemployment rate was north of six percent.[3]

Numerous prospective voters encountered the false claims and their attitudes toward the President became tainted. When they shared that information with their neighbors, they may have seen themselves as patriots, helping those neighbors make better decisions during election day.

A significant point about misinformation is that its consequences are typically the result of something innocent. The source of the information does not generally intend to drive you toward BCDs based on the erroneous information. Disinformation, however, is a term for facts alleged even when the source knows such facts to be wrong. In simple terms, they are lies manufactured to rearrange BCDs.

Like all the threats to your judgments discussed in this chapter, misinformation and disinformation plague your thinking only to the extent that they are abundant. Yet their abundance in our culture is frightening. *The Washington Post* estimates that one recent President of the United States (intentionally or not) told 30,570 lies throughout his four years in office.[4] Suppose those who counted made 10,000 errors in their own review of that President's lies. We are still left with a flood of polluted media consumed by millions of voters.

It is safe to believe that Russian trolls on Twitter ("X") are committed to creating instability and election results favorable to Russia. In 2018, At least 40,000 users retweeted messages from accounts confirmed to be Russian bots 80,000 times. Most of these retweets came from two southern states --- Texas and Tennessee.

---

[3] https://econofact.org/factbrief/did-us-unemployment-fall-to-the-lowest-rate-in-50-years-under-biden
[4] https://www.washingtonpost.com/politics/2021/01/24/trumps-false-or-misleading-claims-total-30573-over-four-years/

Texans shared more than 26,000 Russian tweets and Tennesseans shared nearly 50,000, as described by PBS News.[5]

The website *Carbon Brief*, created in 2020, showcases an excellent discussion of the sources of both misinformation and disinformation designed to create confusion and anger in the general population. Here is an excellent analysis of the variety, persistence, and scope of a single industry group desirous of shaping your view of climate change.[6]

The fossil fuel industry uses funds from corporations with vested interests in climate change to discourage governmental action attempting to reduce the use of fossil fuel. This money goes to political and religious organizations, favorable scientists and online groups masquerading as grassroots organizations. People in positions of power, such as politicians and influential bloggers, repeat and spread this information. In 2022, oil and gas companies and associations spent more than $125 million lobbying against efforts to reduce the use of fossil fuel.

WELL-INTENTIONED BUT SLOPPY THINKING

Many people push others to follow their advice to eat certain foods, sleep particular amounts, exercise in specific ways, and live in one place or another. They believe they have dependable advice and want to share it. However, the quality intentions to assist someone else may vary from the quality of the advice.

For example, many of us have been told that each of us has an especially productive way to learn. Teachers are urged to redesign their classrooms to take advantage of individual best practices. "Some learn best from visual stimuli; others learn optimally from repetition… many learn best from hands-on exercises." The advice

---

[5] https://www.pbs.org/newshour/science/inside-the-study-showing-conservatives-retweeted-russian-trolls-30-times-more-often-than-liberals
[6] https://www.carbonbrief.org/guest-post-how-climate-change-misinformation-spreads-online/

seems plausible, and the fact that it originates from well-meaning sources makes it especially credible.

But unfortunately for this well-meaning advice, a 2009 group of psychologists reviewed eight decades of research studies attempting to find evidence for the belief that a person's learning style is a powerful determinant of how well a person learns. The summary of their search is that as a generalization, learning styles are unrelated to how much we learn. Certain individuals do learn best when classrooms reflect a specific learning style, but for most learners, other factors are a more powerful stimulus.[7]

Bad advice is everywhere, and the good intentions of the advisor do not improve its quality:

- Parents may say, "When will I be a grandmother?" in a not-so-subtle effort for their children to procreate sooner rather than later. But some of us realize that having a child would not be a good idea for either me or the baby. I may not be mature enough now to do well as a parent.

- Mentors often encourage us to go to college where they studied. But I need a college that is much smaller than the campus you attended. I want my teachers to know me when I walk across campus. I have noticed that I have this need, and a larger campus would be a nightmare.

- "Why don't you become an accountant?" Great advice for some, but I break into a cold sweat at the very thought of the numbers in a balance sheet.

- "Strong people never quit." Imagine all the possible situations when you should always quit. Suppose I found myself in a criminal conspiracy that had begun as an honest, legal business. Quitting now may make sense. Alternatively, maybe I took a job as a door-to-door salesperson, but every time customers open the door, I

---

[7] https://www.edweek.org/leadership/learning-styles-arent-a-reliable-way-to-categorize-students-study-says/2018/12

am helpless to do anything but giggle... Thanks for trying to help, but I do not think selling is for me.

SUMMARY

We live in an environment that is often hostile. Especially troublesome are skilled persuaders who desirous of your time, loyalty, and money. Some of them have no intent to harm you, but many are trying to manipulate you for their interests and needs.

Critical thinking is your protector. In learning to ask the questions encouraged in this book, you have taken massive steps toward carefully shielding yourself from those who are propelling you toward major life mistakes.

Most of us understand the importance of personal hygiene. While we may or may not wash our hands with regularity, brush our teeth after every meal, or avoid coughing on others when we are ill, we know that unwelcome infections are lurking in our environment, ready to pounce.

The CDC warns us that poor hygiene can cause unpleasant encounters with athlete's foot, body lice, chronic diarrhea, pinworms, scabies and ringworm. We are generally taught at an early age by parents to protect ourselves by a few healthy hygiene habits.

But what about the threat to our beliefs, conclusions, and decisions (BCDs) when we allow habitual mental flaws to govern our thinking? Neither physical nor mental health come automatically. Somehow, either from coaching or modeling, we must understand and counter the threats to our effective functioning.

Critical thinking is polishing our minds and applying a sealant on top of what we have learned to protect ourselves from pervasive self-deception and error.

CHAPTER TWO

THE FOUNDATIONAL IMPORTANCE OF THE QUESTIONS "WHY?" AND "WHEN?"

One can see this book as a gift that one must learn to appreciate. In other words, to be excited about receiving the gift, the recipient must understand the function of critical thinking in our lives. We want to convince you that acquiring critical thinking skills lets you see with powerful magnification and knowing that what you see is yours to shape. With critical thinking, you can resist the temptations of sloppy thinking by exercising your newfound mental habits.

In this book, "critical thinking" means **a collection of questions we need to ask in search of the quality of reasons and evidence used to justify a BCD**. However, there are also certain questions that are both simple to ask and especially powerful for acquiring the range and depth of information needed to resist the seductive lure of being led to BCDs that serve other's aims. The questions "Why?" and "When?" are particularly powerful but also deceptively simple and basic. Our thinking takes a giant leap forward when we automatically ask these two questions when considering whether to accept a BCD as our own.

WHY? The Sound of Curiosity

A question is one person's request for another to bring light where darkness has ruled. In other words, it is an invitation to a conversation.

Perhaps the most fundamental critical thinking skill is the curiosity activator "Why?" From the age of two, we build our understanding of our world with a constant barrage of requests for reasons. During that period of our lives, we are not concerned by bothering companions as we pepper them with questions.

We are not yet aware that others form judgments about us based on the direction of our wonder; we are not ashamed to admit ignorance in the presence of others. In our early years, we simply want to learn and are comfortable with the image of an explorer.

At that early age, we do not realize that something called an "argument" is constructed based on the responses to our questions, but we soon learn that consequences flow from asking "Why?" We do not seek factoids to win trivia contests, we are forming patterns that will inform choices defining our identity. The meaning of our lives emerges from the answers we form to questions such as:

- How should I divide my time between things that benefit me personally versus those that reflect empathy for others?
- Which of the many political perspectives, from free market capitalism to democratic socialism, will shape my dedication to ideals such as compassion, freedom, or equality?
- Which, if any, of the thousands of religions in the world (each with its creation story, narrative about how the world ends, and expectations for how believers should live), should I embrace?
- To what extent will I seek help from others or rely on my own thoughts to solve problems?
- When I say, "I want to be happy," do I think of obtaining my wants or only my needs?

Habitually asking "Why?" gives us information we need for arriving at a stronger BCD. Critical thinkers neither applaud nor reject a

BCD until they have asked why the proponent wants them to believe it. Asking "Why?" is a request for the foundation on which a BCD sits. When the foundation for a BCD is rotting with termite damage, we must look elsewhere for things to believe in.

The point here is that critical thinking is ambiguous toward a BCD until one considers the reasons for that BCD. To see what our lives would be like without regularly asking "Why?", imagine what believing would mean if we all swapped BCDs simply because we like variety, or because we heard about the newest BCD from a podcast. Critical thinking has a radar focus on the quality of the answer to "Why?"

Because the "Why?" question is so important to careful thinking, it deserves a key role in this book. When we lack wonder about our world or are taught that asking the "Why?" is weird or annoying, conversation dries up, into a desert in which innovative ideas and wise BCDs cannot grow.

It requires strong character and immense drive to re-learn to ask "Why?" or virtually any question that requires reflection or makes someone uneasy. Most of us need active encouragement to risk being someone who asks "too many questions" or, even worse, makes someone else rethink a BCD they hold dear.

Many of us crave acceptance and constantly asking the why question without understanding how to keep a conversation going can lead to being "that" person. Critical thinkers must have the courage to be a missionary on behalf seeking better BCDs in a rigorous, but still courteous, way.

WHEN? The Accuracy or Wisdom of a BCD Depends on the Situation

The second foundational critical thinking question is "When?"

Late in his brilliant life, Einstein was allegedly asked what insight he most desired humanity to have. His response was "Everything is contextual." In other words, the accuracy or truth of a BCD depends on what we learn when we ask "When?"

Instead of considering context, our minds are persistently in a rush. When we learn a superstar athlete is arrested for sexual assault, we are confused. We worshiped his skill as an athlete. We admired his hard work, seeing his success as a model of character for our children. In the aftermath of his crimes, we are dumbfounded.

We think of one another as kind or mean, careful or sloppy, skilled or bumbling, a good or a bad person. But as Einstein says, any BCD you form is only true sometimes, in some situations. Serial killers behave hideously but may also care for their beloved pets or be a thoughtful neighbor. We must ask "When?" so we do not confuse "sometimes" with "always."

Another way to think about the "When?" question is to consider the concept of generalization. Suppose you listened to a podcast by a researcher who discussed her take on the history of three Native American tribes. Her research revealed that these tribes had enormous respect for buffalo and the water sources from which the buffalo thrive. You hear the podcast and tell a friend that you wish our culture paid as much respect for animals and other natural resources as the Native Americans do.

A strong generalization tends to imply "all." If you told your family the above based on the narrative you heard, you have concluded that Native Americans are more respectful of the environment than we are. In doing so, you suggest that the habits of three Native American tribes are shared by _all_ Native American tribes. But a strong generalization is rarely true. We tend to exaggerate the accuracy of generalizations and, in doing so, miss problematic parts of a BCD.

For example, while many Native American tribes were excellent stewards of the environment, some tribes burned large swaths of forest to force out hundreds of elk and deer, though they needed only a fraction of the animals they butchered for subsistence. Similarly, other tribes throughout the Pacific Northwest used elaborate schemes to drive herds of white-tailed deer into forest enclosures, where they were slaughtered in numbers far greater than necessary.

Many generalizations are accurate most of the time. In other words, they are likely correct. Moreover, they can be justified or falsified by statistics indicating just how true and accurate they are.

Hence, such generalizations are weak ones --- although often fair and accurate, in other instances they are false exaggerations. For example, "Young people run faster than older people," is usually true, but there are many instances making this statement a horrible claim as far as strong generalizations go.

Relating back to the importance of context, notice that not all old people are comparatively slow runners. On any weekend, you could likely attend a local 5K race where people in their 50s outrun most runners in their teens.

THE TRUTH OF MANY BCDS DEPENDS ON A VAST ARRAY OF CONTEXTS. An arranged marriage can be a major mistake or a love story for the ages. Training for a particular career may make sense before the invention of AI but could become a ticket to your parents' basement when AI renders your training obsolete.

IT JUST DEPENDS.

CHAPTER THREE

THE RELEVANCE OF MISSING INFORMATION

Human decision making is haunted by an inescapable flaw. It occurs because we are aware of only bits and pieces of the bigger picture of pertinent information. As Exhibit 3-1 suggests, we often think we are ready to make a decision when we know <u>something</u> about the avenue to the conclusion. But there is always so much more to know. Grandpa here knows he has done something related to modern technology skills, but we know he needs to learn a lot more before certifying himself an expert.

Exhibit 3-1

We cannot know everything we need to know about every factor of a decision that could move the needle toward a "Yes," "No," or "Maybe." However, learning certain kinds of information leads to improved choices from among the BCDs others urge us to adopt.

Because of their power spotting flawed arguments and revealing further information, our most fundamental critical thinking habits are asking "Why? and "When?" There are many critical thinking questions, but no others have the liberating power of these two.

Exhibit 3-2

Both questions are attempts to avoid making mistakes. When the answers to the two questions contain nothing that inspires confidence that a BCD is reliable or reasonable, we should remain skeptical until we obtain additional information.

That additional information takes one of two forms that will be the substance of the remainder of the book. Before we can seriously consider a BCD someone wishes us to accept, we need many kinds of information that can push us toward or away from the BCD.

Much of that missing information must be uncovered because it is currently hiding from us. Once uncovered, it must be compared to superior information. Sometimes, we can only rely on information that is less than terrific. A useful general rule is: "The greater the impact on our lives a BCD has, the more we will need to gather fresh, dependable information."

We sometimes rely without hesitation on BCDs even when we're not moved by their truth value. For example, if a friend tries to persuade me to use their favorite brand of toothpaste, I do not need to apply my most careful critical thinking to that suggestion. Unless a toothpaste will destroy your oral health with some fatal flaw, that decision has almost zero importance. You might just buy the suggested toothpaste as a gesture of friendship, or you might ignore the advice until your friend forgets the conversation.

On the other hand, when someone tells you what you should adopt as your life's vocation, the flow of information through which you sift should last many hours.

EVIDENCE

Suppose we told you that one of the most dangerous aspects of living is eating, and when you asked us for our reasoning, we responded, "Just because" or "I simply feel that way." Why would you likely doubt what we said? Would you be more convinced if I presented a study from *Scientific American* concluding that each year unsafe food causes more than 600 million cases of illness from eating those foods, resulting in 420,000 deaths worldwide?

Evidence refers to many things designed to move you from doubt to belief. In the absence of evidence, the most we could expect to accomplish is newfound curiosity. But evidence takes many forms. Some should not move us toward a BCD, while other forms of evidence encourage us toward acceptance.

Let's look at several types of potentially useful evidence, focusing on their merits and drawbacks as information:

HEARSAY

The most dangerous type of evidence is probably "I heard it somewhere," or "I saw it online." Relying on such evidence would make everything true in that it is hard to imagine *anything* that has never been said or heard. Millions of people telling you that the moon landing is a hoax is evidence only of an unfortunate failure by those people to rely on credible expertise.

As the important experiments of Solomon Asch demonstrated, humans tend to conform to BCDs expressed by a group, even when they know the BCD is wrong. We are eager to engage in "groupthink," conforming to information we receive from groups of people even when we know it is wrong. We want to fit in and often lack the courage to offset that inclination with what our senses tell us in contrast.

Observing Asch's experiments unfold is frightening because, after a group announces that it sees seven objects on a table, an individual will announce agreement with the group even when knowing that only six objects are on the table. Critical thinkers need courage to voice their perceptions. One way to find this courage is to realize that groups of knowledgeable humans have been making mistakes for as long as we have been forming BCDs.

Information the public gets from medical research is some of the most carefully analyzed data in the world. Yet the research of John Ioannidis suggests that within three years after such data appears in the top three medical journals in the world, replication studies have refuted it. Consequently, false information in medicine has endangered millions of people.

We owe immense gratitude to physicians and other scientists who have spoken out about erroneous information. Think of the dedication to accurate information by Dr. Ignaz Semmelweis, who singlehandedly changed the behavior of surgeons with three words: "Wash your hands." In the mid-1800s, the leading cause of maternal mortality in Europe was puerperal (also known as "postpartum") fever. Surgeons would go directly from doing an autopsy with their bare hands to delivering babies with the same unwashed hands. Puerperal fever quickly followed.

Dr. Semmelweis' career was severely damaged by the resistance to the behavior he was urging. However, his devotion to truth saved hundreds of thousands of lives and continues to do so today. In instances like this, critical thinking liberates us from deadly ignorance.

Social media permits both falsehoods and life-saving information to spread with dazzling speed. We always need to examine the quality of hearsay information. Six billion of us use the internet, guaranteeing that whatever you heard there has been said multiple times and replicated on the internet by many people.

Once statements are repeated on the internet, they acquire echoes with incredible speed. In that context, rumor can race around the world before truth can get its pants on. Therefore, until we know more about the people who are trying to persuade us, we should not be impressed because seven or even 70 people said the same thing. We have a dangerous tendency to be impressed because a crowd said something. Defend yourself by asking, "How strong is the evidence for that hearsay evidence?"

SURVEY RESULTS

We often are impressed by data from surveys. Such evidence fits with our sense that the opinions of large numbers of people are, at face value, more convincing than information from a few people. And, if carefully gathered, survey evidence can justifiably move us toward a BCD.

However, survey data has multiple potential problems. For one thing, we have all had experience with survey questions that are confusing. Most of us have had an experience on the telephone with customer service or after making a purchase at the store when we are asked to rate the experience from one to ten. Pile that kind of evidence five feet tall and what do you have? A lot of confusion. The people who answer that survey all have different meanings for what a desirable experience is. Some of us are annoyed by the length of the survey and adjust our rating downward. Respondents are sometimes having a bad day when they make their rating and adjust the experience downward as a result. Others had been told yesterday that their cancer is in remission, and in the glow of that news, they may well rate everything as perfect.

As a critical thinker, you will always be curious about the extent to which the information was created using wording that meant the same thing to all respondents.

Another potential problem with survey responses is that the information came from leading questions. Those questions propel the respondent to answer in a particular way. In other words, those who created the survey wish to doctor your responses, moving them in a particular direction. An example of a leading question is, "How has your experience in high school changed your life for the better?" The answers to that question would lead in a different direction from answers to the following question: "How has your experience in high school harmed your view of humans?"

When you see leading questions in a survey, rest assured that someone is intentionally pushing you to a particular BCD. A red alert should go off in your mind warning you to resist the BCD that the survey creators are selling until more reliable information suggests otherwise.

STATISTICS

One of our most important forms of evidence is statistics. They are crucial information in numerical form at the heart of important information which is responsible for advances in science, business, medicine, and public policy creation. But statistics are organized by humans, and as such, they are capable of being highly deceptive.

On day one of a year-long training experience in advanced statistics, one of our professors told the class: "Good morning. Let's learn how to make these numbers sing the song we want to hear." Skilled users of statistics can organize and use statistics to sell a particular BCD. Fortunately, that attitude is not the norm among statisticians. However, critical thinkers need to use caution when encountering statistics.

Perhaps the most common problem you encounter when interpreting statistics is confusion of causation with correlation. Causes precede results. They usually occur near each other. Being alert to the potential confusion between cause and effect in statistical analysis will protect you from problematic BCDs.

Suppose a town is concerned that they have no arson investigators in their community. After hiring two fire investigators, the town council is confused because arson reports jumped 600 percent after the fire investigators were hired. Considering this data, the city council discussed trying to reduce arson in the community by replacing at least one of the arson investigators with a new director of the town's senior center. We are sure you see the error the council may be making. Eyes trained to see an occurrence are much more likely to see the occurrence in larger amounts than would be seen by an untrained eye.

If you found data showing that mental illness has increased immensely during the same period as the increase in trained therapists, you would want to study the potential for confusing correlation and causation before you decided that your community needs more or fewer therapists. Alternatively, you would want to consider information that an increasingly insecure future caused by climate change and sharp inequality might be causing both the number of therapists and the amount of mental illness to increase.

Statistics is a complex and important form of information that deserves attention from all of us. Here we are just touching on its complexity.

The following are a few additional, important problems that can taint statistical information:

- Averages exist in three forms. One is the mean or the sum of the measurements you are making divided by the number of measurements. Another is the mode or the size of the measurement that occurs most frequently in the collection of measurements. A third average is the median or the measurement that separates the higher half from the lower half of a sample of measurements. When you see information in the form of an average, remember that what is reported as an average was quite possibly chosen to encourage a specific BCD.

- "Gee Whiz" graphs are created by making a chart that suddenly rises or falls dramatically to create the effect desired by the people who organized the statistics. An American President once went on television to denounce the tax proposals of his opponents. One line on a graph was very high; the other was very low. The high one was labelled "Their Taxes" and the low one was named "Our Taxes." The next day, the *Washington Post* pointed out that the tax proposals were almost identical. The picture on the graph was created by failing to place any information on the two bars of the graph. Hence, even the smallest difference could be represented as huge.

- Statistics are usually based on relatively few measurements, only a sample of the total of what is being measured. Large samples are expensive and a headache to collect. The temptation to use a small sample and generalize from it can be overwhelming.

- Another sample problem can be failing to design the sample to represent the proportion of the population. For example, to understand how many Americans express a feeling of loneliness, we would want our sample to have the same proportion of teenagers as the proportion in the population. If we failed this standard, we could easily under- or over-count the extent of loneliness.

An additional sample problem is the possibility of dramatic outliers. When one or a few outliers are in the sample we are analyzing, the story the statistics show will be distorted.

PERSONAL EXPERIENCE

At first glance, it might seem that personal experience can never be a reliable basis for embracing a BCD. Why would we think that a single instance of something would provide the basis for a useful generalization? However, our personal experiences are much more than a single instance.

Because they are <u>our</u> experiences, we blow them up into a huge balloon that can almost never pop. We attach a much greater weight to our experiences than we associate with the experiences of others. We insist that we know exactly what we saw, heard, smelled, felt, and tasted, and that we know the meaning of those experiences. As a wonderful book title says, *Mistakes Were Made, But Not by Me.*

A strong illustration of the failure of personal experience to be accurate is testimonial evidence in legal cases. The important work of Elizabeth Loftus has documented over and over that what we believe we experienced is often severely flawed. Juries often rely on eyewitness testimony as convincing. Yet research study after research study has revealed the error of that belief.

Robert A. Burton has persuasively argued that even our understanding of who we are is unreliable. He suggests that when we want to know who we are, our best bet is to ask a wise friend how they would describe us. However, we read Burton's evidence in this regard and generally refuse to believe it. We oversell the accuracy of our personal judgments.

INTERVIEWS AND CASE STUDIES

Interviews and case studies permit us to explore detailed information. As evidence, they have great potential but equally great hurdles. Among the problems presented by interview evidence, perhaps the most serious potential inadequacy is that the persons being interviewed are trying to impress the interviewer.

Consider the job interview. One of us was involved in dozens of hiring decisions. Those of us doing the hiring took our task very seriously; we were "selecting future colleagues." We were certain that some interviewers are much more skilled than others. To improve our judgments from interviews, we discussed the criteria we would be using to design the interviews and knew that the candidates had every reason to be creative when fashioning their answers. We had all read the evidence that 30 percent of those applying for the available positions included on their resumes university degrees that they had never earned. The candidates correctly realized that most interviewers would naively assume that resumes provide accurate information.

Despite what we thought was our due diligence as interviewers, we learned over the course of several decades of experience that applicants often outsmarted us. The person we met in the interview was rarely the successful candidate who showed up to start working with us.

Interview bias is another problem that can damage the usefulness of interviews as reliable evidence. The people doing the interviews may have unconscious biases that interfere with a fair, merit-based assessment of candidates.

Case studies use formats like those used in interviews. They permit greater depth than other forms of evidence often possess. However, they are inescapably subjective. The person doing the exploration has biases that can unintentionally crawl into the interpretation and meaning of what is said by the person being studied.

Case studies are difficult to repeat and, consequently, as information they lack the importance of doing replications as a check on the generalizations derived from interviews. Case studies are very time-consuming and therefore expensive. Nevertheless, when they are done by a skilled interviewer who is explicit about their own possible biases, they can be highly illuminating.

One conclusion that can be drawn from the many evidential sources of information is the desire that a perfect world has information drawn from as many forms of evidence as possible. When we do not have access to multiple forms of evidence, our judgments are necessarily risky.

SOURCES

BCDs are the children of particular parents. The characteristics of those parents tell you important information you need before you can use the information. Some sources are skilled consumers of information with a desire to enhance our knowledge. At the other extreme are those who will do or say almost anything to move your BCDs in a particular direction.

Each of us must rely on the expertise of others every day. But all authorities are not equally reliable sources. Some sources are so uninformed about knowledge they claim to possess that you should be especially attentive to examining whatever BCDs they are offering you. The following exhibit provides you with protective filters warning you when a source tells you that you should make a BCD yours.

When we are not careful, we are overly impressed by claims that "Studies show..." or "Careful research reveals..." The elements in Exhibit 3-3 enable you to discover whether an expert has earned the respect that gives credibility to the psychological forces being used in the previous sentence. We need studies and careful research, but failing to make use of the questions in the chart below enables superficial reasoning.

One popular syndicated disc jockey describes recently published data between songs. We have no reason to think that the intention of the disc jockey is anything other than benefiting their listeners. Repeatedly, the results of the quoted study are expressed with a kind of "Gee-whiz!" excitement that is seductive. We want information and here is someone giving us some. But, alas, the disc jockey acts as if whatever is published in any source is newly revealed, reliable information. Such naivete can produce a situation where new information is harmful.

DEFINITIONS

Our primary communication device is words. Our so-called "second language" consists of the many things we do with our body, hands and face that have communicative effects. When we use these tools, we tend to know what message we are sending. However, our language is complicated. What you have said may well not be what I heard.

Exhibit 3-4

The problem that results from these communication failures is complicated. Initiators of a communication believe understandably that they can proceed with more words or behavior based on a common meaning of whatever word they use. But important missing information taints the effort to communicate.

Suppose a teenager wishes to borrow the family car one weekend evening. Mother says, "Yes, if you study a lot the rest of the week." Study? Their agreement is as clumsy as an international negotiation when the parties agree to "Peace," but each means: "Assuming you agree to the preconditions I have consistently announced."

Study? The teenager assumes that studying with the television on will satisfy the precondition for a fun weekend with the family car. Mom meant by "study" the same thing her parents always meant --- television off. But that verbal ambiguity is only the beginning of the problem. The teenager assumed that even one more hour of additional study would qualify as adequate. Mom would never have meant that tiny bit of extra "study" would deserve access to the family car.

Words have multiple meanings, and as a critical thinker you will want to identify the key words that need clarification and ask which meaning of those words is intended. Here are a few statements for you to practice clarifying ambiguity. Just ask yourself what information you would need, in the form of definitions, to be certain about what is being said:

- I asked my wife how much money I would need to earn for her to be proud of me.
- Can I live at home after I graduate from college?
- You should see the new film with Justin Timberlake starring in it. I hear it is the best movie of the year.

Even a seemingly transparent word like "cow" contains multiple meanings. When we say the word, our previous experiences associated with the word or phrase in question shapes what we mean by "cow." When one of us says "cow" he is relying on a decade of experience with dairy cows on his grandparents' farm. To him, they were a source of beauty. He stared often into their large, incredible eyes and hoped he could someday create art with such beauty. But for someone else, it is highly understandable for "cow" to signal impending danger. An angry bull can scare you as thoroughly as can an angry momma elephant.

But let's get real. This degree of clarity in what we hear or say would require more time than we can generally spare for that purpose. Therefore, critical thinkers will ask to clarify ambiguity only when the word in question contains multiple meanings that would alter the direction of the argument.

RELEVANCE

Remember that the support offered for the truth or effectiveness of a BCD is the focus of critical thinking. But sometimes an argument makes no sense at all. Imagine, for example, that someone urges you to buy a four-foot iguana to take a better nap. What could that possibly mean? In this case the persuasion process is so mysterious that we cannot even see how it would be possible to respond. Asking something like, "Could you help me understand how having an iguana of that size helps one enjoy a nap?" is a courteous, discovery-oriented response. However, by itself, the link between the two events is nonsensical.

Let's look at a more complicated illustration of the importance of the relevance of information. Suppose an aunt urged you to drop out of school and the rationale she provided for that major decision was that she had recently purchased another cute Vietnamese pig. You stare at the reason offered for why you should drop out of school, and you see no avenue by which it has anything to do with your school plans. In other words, you do not see the relevance of the reason to the conclusion.

Reasons that are not pathways to a BCD leave you scratching your head. "Please be my friend. I am 90 years old." Okay, but why are you telling me your age? As you think about this section regarding the relevance of new information, you may think that no one uses arguments like the two illustrations above. But if you listen closely, you will frequently hear irrelevant support.

This section is more useful than it may seem. The spirit of critical thinking is one of discovery and growth. New information has the potential to liberate you from repeating previous mistakes. That potential is not activated when we reply to seemingly irrelevant support for a BCD by rolling your eyes or just repeating your opposition to the BCD.

Critical thinking works best when it demonstrates respect for the person with whom you are talking. When we treat the other person as confused or silly, we discourage the person from using critical thinking because it seems unkind. The basic idea of this entire chapter is that we enhance our thinking when we acquire information that we had lacked prior to the encounter with another person. Premature allegiance to a BCD is a dangerous habit.

Therefore, try to react to seemingly irrelevant information by asking the other person to help you understand their thinking. "Why do you think that it makes sense to link buying a pig to whether to continue in school?" If the other person realizes the strangeness of what they said, you should be quick to point out that you too sometimes say things that surprise you after thinking more about it. The idea of that kind of response is to model a friendly form of critical thinking.

When you ask for clarification of a seemingly bizarre statement, you may surprise yourself with the information you gain. Suppose your request for more information disclosed the following: "I knew that your current school experience was discouraging you from throwing yourself into your mental growth. I think you may know that I own a firm that purchases Vietnamese pigs and trains them to be pets for the local senior center. Each pig requires a single trainer, or they are virtually untrainable. I thought you might want to train my new pig as a temporary stopping point in your life. Depending on the experience, you might want to join me in the pet pig business or find a schooling opportunity that better matches your needs and motivations."

The new information revealed here may provide strong support for the eventual decision about whether you should stay in school. But if the search for new information had been abbreviated after hearing the "reasoning" for the first time, you may have never known the opportunity you were being offered.

The message in the following exhibit is that when you hear something that seems irrelevant, the only way to be sure and to treat the other person with respect is to extend the search politely.

Exhibit 3-5

NUMBERS

In *Filters against Folly*, eminent biologist Garrett Harden claimed that much insight could be revealed by using numbers as often as possible to clarify elements in an argument. The support for a BCD as well as the BCD itself can be enriched by the precision enabled by numbers. Harden urged us to be "numerate," i.e., to use numbers when they bring precision to our understanding. To be numerate is to habitually pay attention to counts, weights, ratios, rates of change and proportions.

Certain words shout out "Numbers, please." For example, when a comparison is expressed between two brands of pickles, three sushi restaurants, or two treatments for skin cancer, the alleged superior choice is always said to be "more" desirable than the other options. In the next chapter, we will learn that this argument is "begging the question." To "beg" a question is to pretend to provide a reason or explanation, fail to do so because your explanation does not advance our understanding of your thinking. On the contrary, while it poses as an explanation, what was offered as an explanation is merely asking the same question but in other words. Only the second time the question is asked a word like "better" is replaced by the words "more desirable." We are left with a conclusion and no reasoning to support it.

But what are the numbers and what do they mean? How much better is the choice claiming to be superior? Is the difference major or is it so close that in effect they are equally desirable? Is the measure of superiority using the same understanding of "more" that you would use when making these comparisons? If the differences reveal one superior choice, why were the numbers used to explain that superiority not included in the reasoning supporters provided? If large numerical measures of superiority did exist, would its supporters not have included the numbers?

Another word that would ideally be expressed in numbers is "improves." As all television viewers know, medicines and other medical treatments are sold as if they are miracles waiting to be experienced.

The Mayo Clinic tells us that many people find that acupuncture improves their insomnia, depression, stress, migraines, energy levels, allergies, blood pressure problems, digestion, neck pain and as well as dozen other additional discomforts. But what are the numbers? What is the percentage or proportional impact? Before I schedule my acupuncture appointment, just how much, on average, does it reduce high blood pressure? Furthermore, what is the improvement from comparative treatment between acupuncture and any of several drugs like Prinivil that focus on blood pressure?

Under U.S. law, there is no numerical standard of effectiveness (no number for rate of improvement) about which a patient can truly be confident. FDA testing is very extensive and rigorous, but drugs with almost zero effectiveness are also approved, prescribed, and sold. While the complexity of efficacy measures prohibits a single standard for how much a drug reduces a medical condition, potential users have good reason to stay knowledgeable about the latest information concerning a drug's effectiveness.

Anytime an idea can be measured and explained, the relevant numbers need to be explored before acting on the ambiguity associated with claims of medical effectiveness. The same caution applies to the importance of all numbers that can more precisely represent the extent or measurement of an element of a BCD or the support offered for the BCD advocated.

FUTURE IMPACTS

Another element critical thinkers should examine when evaluating an argument is the tendency of action to stimulate additional actions in a possible ongoing chain of events. For example, in the midst of a bloody war, it is tempting for the nation controlling airspace to bomb its enemy into oblivion. However, every dead enemy body creates a string of impacts that may last for generations.

The United States once had an Air Force general who advocated bombing Vietnam into a parking lot; years later, a Marine Corps general advocated as a solution to airplane hijacking that we should place the mother of a hijacker on a tarmac tied to two airplanes headed in opposite directions and then having the airplanes pull the lady into pieces.

What kind of madness were these two generals voicing?

First, the suggestions are ethically disgusting, but what the generals were doing is a dramatic illustration of the failure to appreciate "ecolacy," the realization that we can never do just one thing. Any decision we make has effects that go far beyond the initial outcome. Garrett Hardin discussed our habit of remembering that there are secondary (second) and tertiary (third) impacts from any action taken in our environment. We can extend the concept to any act or failure to act that we take as humans to solve a problem.

For example, we can slay an opponent, but that opponent may have grandchildren and grandchildren of grandchildren. Treat current generations as if they are less than human, and you risk fueling intergenerational revenge that is difficult to eradicate.

Failure to examine the information flowing from human actions applies to our species at many levels. We harvest rainforests for building material for a growing population observing the relative luxury of wealthy countries. However, have we identified the kind of world we will have as the rainforests shrink?

We support politicians who promise to cut our taxes. Naturally enough, most of the resulting tax cuts give the largest breaks to the richest people. The top one percent of wealth-holders own one-third of the world's wealth. The richest ten percent of Americans own more wealth than the remaining 90 percent of the U.S. population. These numbers are controlled by humans, and can therefore be revised by humans. The laws that permit the inequality are an occurrence with unending effects on the quality of schools, health care, the environment, and hope.

As a critical thinker, we must realize that our behavior has impacts that live on and on. Therefore, we want to embrace BCDs only after we have reminded ourselves that the lifespan of an action extends far beyond the immediate consequences. Asking questions to identify probable information about secondary and tertiary effects is a public service.

Because none of us can ever acquire all the information that would be available in a perfect world, we need to recognize that <u>any additions</u> we can make by critical thinking leads to a more thoughtful set of BCDs.

SUMMARY

Information is the potential creator of wise BCDs.

Imagine that we told you that your family needs to purchase at least three of something called *syots* because they are essential protection against the many severe weather catastrophes that threaten our safety. We deliver to you a pamphlet of reviews praising the desirability of possessing at least three *syots*.

Certainly, we would all like to have anything that would enhance the safety of our loved ones. While you probably know little about *syots*, and we all have BCDs that we embraced before we even know about *syots* at all. Now that you have read this chapter, think of the many questions that you know should be answered before you run to Amazon to place a new order.

- How were those reviews obtained? Was there a benefit to the reviewers from urging others to buy *syots*?

- Are the reviewers a reliable source for making judgments about safety from weather catastrophes? Do they have any specialized training in safety from such events? Is their evaluation overseen by other professionals?

- Where I live there are only certain weather-related catastrophes, so what are the numbers indicating the effectiveness of *syots* for each type of weather catastrophe?

- What is the comparable effectiveness and cost of alternatives to *syots*?

- What long-term effects result when we use *syots* for greater safety?

If you need additional support for being a critical thinker, ask yourself, "How much more mistake-prone would my life be if I did not utilize the revelations from additional information gotten via questions like those in this chapter?"

CHAPTER FOUR

MISUSED INFORMATION

An abundance of information is an essential ingredient for careful thinking. When our minds operate with only a limited file of information, we are struggling in a polar landscape with only a skimpy bathing suit to keep us warm. The beliefs you have <u>before</u> you form a BCD are called "assumptions."

However, at the same time, not all information is necessarily beneficial. As the previous chapter tried to make clear, the potential benefits of additional information are a valuable tool only when this information is used with other data. Quantity matters as well as quantity. Tiny amounts of information can cause us to make BCDs prematurely.

In addition, determining the quality of information is a central task of critical thinking. When using information online, for example, we must be aware of the contemporary danger of social media permitting liars, conspiracy peddlers and manipulators polluting our thinking.

For instance, a potentially revealing study can be tainted by a poorly designed sample shape or size, or a cleverly designed interview can produce deceptive information because of interviewer bias. The point here is that the mountains of information from Google guides our thinking in productive patterns only after we have asked critical thinking questions about it.

This chapter begins where the previous one ended. We are aware that information is essential groundwork for informed thinking. We are familiar with the various ways we can gain information and the potential problems each encounters as we search for more and better information. This chapter surveys the difficulties we face when we use the information we have accumulated.

QUESTIONABLE ASSUMPTIONS

When we act on one of our BCDs, we do so with a history embedded in our minds. Our culture taught us long ago that when a person answers a question with a head nodding up and down, the person is saying "Yes." But that assumption is a prelude to a potential disaster if you are selling something to a person from Bulgaria, in whose country head nodding is a definite "No." We can strain to erase that baggage of assumptions we carry with us, but it clings to our mind with an irresistible tenacity.

For example, at even the simplest level, would you follow the advice of an acquaintance who urges you to eat a bowl of seaweed? Over many years, you have developed a preference for a particular diet, and seaweed is maybe not a component of that diet. As such, seaweed might only be roughly as edible to you as a spoonful of gravel.

The BCDs in your background propel you toward particular reactions. As Exhibit 4-1 suggests, because assumptions are embedded deep in our consciousness, becoming aware of them opens our eyes to why we have a particular BCD because we can examine it from a little bit of distance.

Exhibit 4-1

Suppose your family prides itself on the joy of experiencing food from many cultures. In your family, you would be teased for not giving seaweed a try. They might pressure you to eat seaweed by pointing out what you miss due to your negative reaction to seaweed.

A single serving of seaweed can provide 25 percent of the recommended daily quota of Vitamin K. In addition, the many antioxidants in seaweed help the body resist cell damage, such as minerals such as zinc, phosphorus, and potassium, and the Omega-3 fatty acids found in seafoods generally.

Some cultures eat dogs; others eat crickets. How you react to those two menu items is not entirely based on reasons and evidence. Instead, it is based largely on habits. As soon as you heard the invitation to eat seaweed, your prior experiences and the cultural norms you have been taught rush to the fore, pushing you to answer in a particular way.

In so many ways, what we choose today has been molded by what we were taught to believe yesterday. Those preferences have not been written in stone, but they do exist and resist modification. We simply assume that certain facts are true. Critical thinking urges us to ask how reliable these assumptions are.

The point here is that you cannot erase these priors while you decide whether to eat seaweed. Work as hard as you wish to have an open mind, but hidden persuaders have shoved you toward a particular behavior.

We often declare we will be guided by "the facts." However, we forget that which facts we hear and which we ignore, as well as the weight assigned to any one fact, all rest upon layers of assumptions. Try as we might, we cannot set aside the mental baggage we bring to a conversation. To drive home this point, consider how hard it would be for any of us to say, "We live in the 23rd happiest country in the world," even though that ranking is exactly the conclusion of the *World Population Review* from 2024.[8]

Most of us would quickly attempt an all-out critique of the data used to justify such an outrageous claim.

---

[8] https://worldpopulationreview.com/country-rankings/happiest-countries-in-the-world

Critical thinking questions about assumptions are essential to making information useful. First, we ask, "What assumptions are lurking behind the curtains when someone urges us to make a BCD our own?" Next, after we have exposed the major assumptions in an argument, we need to ask, "Is this assumption true?"

Identifying an erroneous assumption can keep us safe and healthy. We would be largely disposed to manipulation by the marketplace if we believed that people attempting to sell us something are truthful. Sometimes they are, and often they are telling partial truths. When someone says, "My friend, you need a new roof," we would respond with, "Thank you for telling me. I will check with four or five other people to see whether you are correct."

When searching for assumptions, a productive start is to decide whether any of these common assumptions have wormed their way into your reasoning:

- If something worked in the past it will work in the future.
- Freedom is always desirable.
- Information is always helpful to careful decision making.
- The world is fair.
- Being positive about the future moves us in the direction of improvement.
- Humans are rational when they make key decisions.
- Humans are basically egotistical, social, generous, honest, or acquisitive.
- Luck is the primary determinant of success.
- The best way to measure human worth is by examining how much money a person has.

- Humans are responsible for what happens to them during their lives.

As you think about the strengths and weaknesses of assumptions like those above, remind yourself that we are examining assumptions not because they are right or wrong, but because they are powerful hidden architects containing elements of both accuracy and half-truths.

CONFUSED LOGIC

To be logical is to reach a BCD only after the support for it leads inescapably to that BCD. For example, it is logical that when I feel swelling or pressure around my eyes or cheeks and my lymph glands are the size of a golf ball, I may have a sinus infection. However, it is not logical to say that I have a sinus infection when my pet bulldog refuses to eat three meals in a row. When something is not logical, we say it makes no sense. When logic is confused, the reasons and BCD have a weak connection.

The best way to identify confused logic is to familiarize yourself with frequent logical fallacies. This chapter familiarizes you with several of the logical fallacies with the hope that you will be stimulated to learn additional fallacies as you search for improved BCDs:

- *Ad Hominem:* "I urge everyone not to vote for Senator Ramirez because he has a Spanish name." The problem with this logic is that a true reason is used to justify a choice of whom to vote for, but the truth of the reason has no relevance to whether a person is a desirable leader. The faulty logic here is the lack of connection between the support offered for the BCD it urges. A person has many characteristics; their beliefs suggest something about whether they are a desirable candidate. The size of their ears or their height have no logical link to the BCD.

- *Bandwagon Fallacy:* "I could not decide which concert to buy tickets for, so I looked at which concert had the most ticket sales and decided to go to the concert that the most people wished to see." The logical failure here would lead us to eat French fries instead of green beans. Following that same logic, we would choose to get our news from whichever platform has the most listeners. Moreover, we might move from our current location to Tokyo because of its population of 37 million.

The confused logic here would lead to a very rigid set of BCDs. In that all choices would obey the conclusion that what is best is whatever most people say is best, there would be no place for growth, imagination or creativity.

- *Appeal to Pity Fallacy:* "I know I have not come to work for three weeks, but please let me have a raise. I have been having horrible nightmares and cannot complete my assignments. But I need the raise because now I am going to have huge medical bills to address my mental illness." Using pity as a justification for providing employment and a raise is an emotional appeal lacking any attention to the reasons a person should have a job or a raise.

If this logic made sense, we might give raises to those who need them most, regardless of the quality of the work the person does. Were appeals to pity a justifiable basis for a raise, anyone who recently experienced a tragedy would immediately receive a raise, and the more horrific the tragedy, the larger the raise would be.

- *Begging the Question Fallacy:* "Our basketball team is the best basketball team because it plays basketball so well." This fallacy contains, as all arguments do, a conclusion and reasons supporting the conclusion. But in this case, the conclusion and the support for it are identical. Someone is still curious about what makes our basketball so great.

After hearing the conclusion and support for the conclusion, the question remains unanswered or "begged." We are told the team plays well and it is the best. But we are not told what makes them so wonderful. Can they jump higher, avoid getting hurt better than other teams, run harder because of superior conditioning, or seize more opportunities with better judgment? Any of those would advance the discussion. Instead, the question and answer were identical.

- *Straw Man Fallacy:* "Rolanda, for optimal health, you should exercise three hours every week." "But Daekwon, I thought the best way to avoid diabetes is to regulate your sugar intake." What Rolanda has done here is claiming that Daekwon said something focused on how to avoid diabetes. Rolanda entirely ignored the argument that Daekwon made about overall health by answering a related question that Daekwon never asked.

This fallacy requires careful listening or reading to notice. It is called "straw man fallacy" because the person being addressed claims that the original speaker said something that is easy to refute, avoiding the BCD truly suggested by the original speaker.

We have all been a frustrated victim of this form of confused logic. We never said what the other person refuted. The best response in this situation is to ask: Do you want to address the question of what is best for our health, or would you prefer to address your question about diabetes first?

- *The Appeal to Authority Fallacy:* "I know you are trying to persuade me to agree with you that we should wash our pillowcases at least once a week because a dermatologist told *TIME Magazine* that each week five million colony-forming units of bacteria per square inch attach to our pillowcase. But I cannot accept your conclusion because it relies on the "appeal to authority" fallacy.

The confused logic here is the claim that a BCD is wrong because someone used a fallacy while touting the BCD. This fallacy is especially important because a key to understanding critical thinking is the realization that it in no way involves the evaluation of a BCD itself. On the contrary, critical thinking is an evaluation of the pathway by which someone wishes us to believe the BCD.

In its current form, this argument is confused logic. But there are perhaps many other possible avenues by which a persuasive and logical case could be made that we need to wash our pillowcases more frequently.

- *Confusing Correlation and Causation:* A cause occurs before its effect or impact. In other words, any cause has a time-link to its result. But many things happen almost immediately before a numerous other events. Exhibit 4-2 might suggest that a rooster stimulates the sun to rise, but we know better. This exhibit provides a reminder that before we decide we know a cause, we need to identify an explanation for how the one event moved the other.

Exhibit 4-2

RIGHT OR WRONG: THE DANGER OF DICHOTOMIZATION

Our minds are comfortable with dichotomies. The simplicity of characterizing a person as kind or mean, of or a nation as generous or stingy, appeals to us. Living in a world in which important questions have answers that are definitively right or wrong comforts us.

We want to know whether car A or car B is responsible for the death of a loved one so we can fasten blame onto one party. The complex web of responsibility detracts us from seeking revenge for the ugly event.

Even highly educated people who should know better are seduced by the fruits of certitude sustained by dichotomous thinking. One of us once spent an entire lecture transfixed by the comments a colleague was writing on his student's exams. Any student who failed to say that increases in the minimum wage would cause increases in unemployment or that increases in taxes reduce overall government revenue received a variant of "You need to take another look at your notes," and a low grade. The "better" students echoed the ideological correct answer and rewarded with "Good work."

However, those right answers are true only in certain contexts. Discussing those contexts and their impact would force us to realize that we do not live in a True/False world. "Maybe" or "It depends" are often more thoughtful descriptions of our beliefs, conclusions, and decisions.

A useful way to think about the sloppiness of dichotomous thinking is analyzing how people answer the question: Should you be religious?

Perry Bacon, Jr. agonized over this question in a recent *Washington Post* opinion piece where he expressed his wish for a surrogate place that could provide him with certain collective benefits --- benefits that he had formerly experienced in the Christian religion.

He is now one of the rapidly growing number of Americans who answer "none" when asked their religious preference.[9]

Religion meets different needs for different people. Some need physical locations where they can join with people who share values, sing anthems, and share unifying experiences. Others feel no need to associate with institutions based on faith-based thinking.

Critical thinking coaxes us to remain open to options and to support institutions that value relevant evidence and habitual rationality.

COGNITIVE BIASES

Cognitive psychologists and neuroscientists have worked to make us more fully aware of how our brains function. Their research has made a major contribution that should humble us in many regards. We've learned that our brains inherently taint our judgments in certain ways that are extremely difficult to avoid, even when we are aware of its many biases. This chapter describes a few of those biases to illustrate the problems they can create. We hoped that this information will spark your interest in learning about more of them.

- *Availability Bias:* "After that news documenting the mid-flight opening of the front door of the plane, I am not going to fly anymore." Entertaining, vivid, or recent events have an exaggerated impact on our thinking. Our memory is selective, and that selectivity is guided by factors that distort our judgment.

- *Effort Justification Bias:* "I am in love with my bookcases; it took me days to figure out how to construct them." As is true of many cognitive biases, their source is our own self-love. Just as we tend

---

[9] https://www.washingtonpost.com/opinions/2023/08/21/leaving-christianity-religion-church-community/

to adore the vacations we plan, anything on which we have spent a lot of time and money is going to garner much more praise than a more objective reaction to the event.

- *Confirmation Bias:* During a break in their chemistry class, three women agree that "The professor is biased against women. Did you notice that she asked three difficult questions in a row to women students?" Think of the many reasons why a professor might ask three difficult questions in a row to women...

The professor wants the class to go as smoothly as possible and believed that those three women were the most likely students to provide thoughtful responses.

The professor calls on students based at random. She would have called on three males in a row had they been next on the professor's roster.

These three women are the only students planning to go to graduate school and she wants them to be better prepared for a graduate program revolving around asking questions.

- *Illusion of Control Bias:* "If we approach problems with a 'can-do' attitude, we will have success." As with many of these biases, there is at least an inch of truth in that adage. To the extent that you have any control over an event, you are less likely to achieve your desires when you expect failure. What is the point of expending a lot of wasted energy?

In general, there are a host of causal factors affecting your life. Hence, it is naïve to see yourself as able to master your future through wish-fulfillment. Genes, weather, illness, historical era in which you exist, contacts, parents, class, race, sex, and just everyday luck affect how much a positive outlook can shape your life.

- *Illusion of Transparency Bias:* "I cannot understand how the electricians I train are unable to apply the training I have provided." When we know something well, it is very difficult to recall what it was like before you learned. The vocabulary you have now is possessed by people with advanced training. When an expert tells a neophyte something, only a single step has been taken up a long staircase of achievement in that field.

- *Status Quo Bias:* "I have a terrific job offer in California, but I am going to stay in New Jersey because I am familiar with this area of the country." We tend to exaggerate the merits of our current choices. In other words, a more rational calculation of changing your life situation would result in a lower estimation of maintaining the status quo than you assign to it.

- *Objectivity Bias:* "When Marian explains what happens with the spread of AI, she always prefaces what she says by claiming her objectivity in forming her opinion." We are notoriously blind to our own biases. We claim that we understand other perspectives and are open to them. We are equally quick to notice the others' biases when they hold a BCD tightly. Research suggests that the most objective we can be is when, as a preface to sharing our opinions, we are open about our biases.

- *Hindsight Bias:* "I have an incredible ability to predict winning horses. When I check the papers, I see that the winning horses are the ones I would have bet on." Believing that we possess unusual skill making predictions based on our success matching the choices we would have made with the ultimate winners is dubious at best.

If I claim amazing accuracy based on my purported hindsight success, would I not be incredibly famous and rich? This bias is one of dozens resulting from our romance with the self. We tend to see many more talents in ourselves than a fair-minded observer would identify.

In summary, our rationality has severe limitations that damage the quality of our reasoning, and the best way to guard against these limitations in the form of cognitive biases is to familiarize yourself with them.

EXAGGERATED SELF-CONFIDENCE

Self-confidence is extraordinarily useful because it gives us strength to grow and experiment with new people and ideas. Critical thinking benefits from self-confidence because it fuels the courage to ask questions. Being asked a thoughtful question is a challenge. When you are asked your name, answering that question is quick and simple. But when someone asks me why I believe that advertisers tell the whole truth and nothing but the truth, I feel tension. First, am I really making that assumption? Second, if I am, do I have enough relevant and reliable information or facts to justify making that assumption? Finally, am I familiar with the reasoning of those who make the contrary assumption? These questions may expose me as the sloppy thinker that I prefer not to acknowledge.

Self-confidence gives me the courage to welcome these questions as a road to better judgment. I realize that I can always be pursuing improved BCDs. My self-confidence allows me to appreciate challenges to my current thinking. Lacking self-confidence, I would simply feel anger and fear of embarrassment that I might have made a mistake.

Long ago, Aristotle emphasized the great virtue of moderation. This value has important implications for thinking about the role of self-confidence in our lives. Extreme forms of self-confidence can be the vigorous enemy of careful thinking.

Arrogance is a rotting form of self-confidence that transforms a personal benefit into a social disease. Exhibit 4-3 gives us a vision of the potential danger from exaggerated self-confidence.

Exhibit 4-3

One way to see the contours of the disease is to see the epidemic of cognitive biases fertilized by arrogance. Commitment bias, for example, is the tendency to stick with our current BCDs despite extensive evidence that they are wrong. We stick with conclusions because changing BCDs would indicate that we made a mistake. We are not eager to reveal our fallibility as humans. "Mistakes were made, but not by me."

Numerous other cognitive biases are rooted in arrogance:

- *IKEA Effect*: We overvalue the quality of things that we have built compared to things made by others.

- *Mere Exposure Effect:* We prefer things with which we are familiar. If we are familiar with something, we tell ourselves that we must have had strong reasons for selecting it in the past.

- *Planning Fallacy:* We persistently underestimate how long it will take to complete a task. Doing so reflects our faith that we are incredibly competent.

DUNNING-KRUGER

Perhaps the clearest picture of the negative impact of arrogance on how we use information is the Dunning-Kruger Effect. Our thinking has an inescapable problem: we do not know what we do not know. In other words, it is highly unlikely that I will seek information if I do not know I need it. Similarly, when I have extensive knowledge in an area, I may exaggerate by presuming I have little to learn in that discipline. Carry this sentiment around, and you have a recipe for long-term neglect of important missing information.

The Dunning-Kruger Effect has a corollary impact on those who are well-trained in a particular craft. Suppose I have been well-trained in the rules of grammar. Consequently, I have greater awareness of the complexities of grammar than most people. When asked to rate my own competence in grammar, I may exaggerate how *little* I know about grammar. My grammar training has reduced my self-appraisal in that area because my knowledge has made me aware of the vastness of its complexity and how much more there is to know. In this case, the result may be feeling that you are an imposter who may be exposed at any moment.

The Dunning-Kruger Effect and other cognitive biases, like those explained in this section, are persistent sources of information abuse. Consequently, careful thinking is usually slow thinking. Critical thinkers acknowledge our dangerous impulse to rapidly form BCDs. As such, always study the BCDs and reasoning of those with whom you disagree.

Critical thinkers pride themselves on their willingness to think <u>with</u> those with conflicting BCDs. Arrogant people hear others speak and quickly shift into thinking <u>against</u> them. Excessively self-confident people interrupt other people in part because they feel that what they have to say is more informed than others trying to speak. But to be interrupted is to feel disrespected.

Arrogance defeats one of the most important precedents to being open to new and abundant information. With arrogance in the room, there is little space for humility. Critical thinking is curious and exploratory because we realize we have so much to learn from others. Exhibit 4-4 reminds us that knowledge speaks, but wisdom listens.

Exhibit 4-4

FLAWED PERCEPTIONS

Events occur; interpretations of events follow. Between those two occurrences resides a system of perceptions. Think of perceptions as access points between the information we believe we possess and an external world of smells, tastes, sounds, sensations, and probably most importantly, recorded light from objects around us that our brains' visual cortex transforms into information.

Perceptions function at multiple levels of sharpness or intensity. Therefore, perceptions' ability to capture the external world varies. In other words, when we say we see something, we are exaggerating the extent of certitude we are referencing. To "see" exists on a spectrum.

In short, perception varies in many ways depending on a vast array of characteristics. The following characteristics also participate in shaping the messages our senses send us, among others:

- The accumulation of experiences that have shaped subsequent perceptions of behavior
- One's age and culture
- The time of day
- Personality variables impacting concentration
- Mood at the time of perception
- Family background
- Climate

Psychologists are the primary specialists in this dimension of critical thinking. That focus is often the reason a discussion of critical thinking in that area of study uses a vocabulary different from that of neuroscientists or philosophers. The remainder of this chapter will highlight contributions emerging from psychology.

Specifically, we will be explaining the critical thinking questions that identify tainted perceptions.

Our psychological drive for certitude manifests extremes in our perceptions. You think of your parents' marriage and label it as secure or crumbling based on one incident. You think of your soccer-playing ability and allow one mistake at a crucial point in a game to cause you to call your skills horrible. In the language of this chapter, you are seeing information as units of extreme perceptions. Therefore, when you use these perceptions as information to form a BCD, you are misusing information.

Another perceptual distortion results from catastrophizing. Consider that your windshield wipers come unglued while you're driving through a rainstorm. Instead of stopping at an auto supply store, installing new wipers, and focusing on the rest of your day, you react to the event like a tsunami threatening to drown a continent. You tell anyone who will listen that your life is one huge disaster. While catastrophizing, any perception you rely on is going to differ noticeably from a perception of the same thing on a day when you are calmly going about living.

You also perceive the world through the prism of a series of "shoulds." There is no room for perceptions deviating from this opinionated perspective. Adults should shower every day; living rooms should not have pictures on the walls that stimulate uncomfortable thoughts; we should all vote for the candidate with military experience. The logic behind our "shoulds" is rarely explained; our obedience to the "should" is more important than exploring their reasonableness. We find that variations from this obedience are not acceptable, despite conditions that rationally suggest that the "should" may need to be relaxed.

Another area in which information lacks situational complexity is the tendency to use labels, not explanations, to express perceptions. For example, when the person hired to mow my lawn is rushed to the hospital after the lawnmower sends a shard of glass at his head, my father explains what happens by labelling the employee a "fool." My father's response dodges responsibility by ignoring how the glass was left in the yard, why the lawnmower we provided had no safety shield, or why my father did not provide safety glasses to prevent injury.

Again, the research of Elizabeth Loftus documents the importance of critical thinking questions regarding eyewitness testimony. Her research focuses on the extent to which perceptions dredged from memories of past events are unreliable. Despite her call for greater understanding of perception errors, hundreds of people every year are convicted of felonies when the prosecution has little to no evidence beyond eyewitness testimony.

APPENDIX ONE

SUMMARY

More information is an inescapable requirement for improved reasoning. When a mind is starved for reliable and true information, support for BCDs is wounded; BCDs then are stunted. However, piles of information alone are not guaranteed to improve reasoning. Enhanced information can unfortunately be misused.

In using information, flawed assumptions can direct reasoning toward erroneous BCDs. Logical flaws in the connective tissue between reasons and BCDs can capture and infect information. Failures to recognize and avoid harmful cognitive biases in the use of an influx of information distorts our reasoning. Exaggerated self-confidence blinds us to conflicting information because once we use other information to form a BCD, we tend to ignore voices urging us to appreciate alternatives. Similarly, reluctance to acknowledge flaws in our perceptions may lead to premature BCD formation.

Information is a tool, and just as a hammer can destroy a hand that was mistaken as a target, information in of itself has no inherent message; we assign it meaning. We use both hammers and information for our purposes. Deploying information objectively is part of the mission of critical thinking.

APPENDIX TWO

INTELLECTUAL BENEFACTORS

We can write this book only because we tried to be attentive to the wisdom of others. Their insights were responsible for any depth we brought to the themes in this book. Our gratitude is immense.

Berger, W. *A More Beautiful Question*, Bloomsbury USA, 2016. Warren Berger's work has played a vital role in sparking interest in the immense power of a probing question. His work is especially valuable for illustrating the broad range of settings where questions inspire and provoke curiosity that extends beyond the initial questions. Because it presents questions as a launch pad for creativity, this book suggests the integrative relationship between critical thinking and creative thinking.

Burton, R.A. *On Being Certain: Believing You Are Right Even When You are Not*, St. Martin's Press, 2008. Humility plays a key role in explaining the need for critical thinking. When humility is absent, learning and specifically asking questions, is a waste of time in that I have already seen truth; it is omnipresent in my mind. Our self-knowledge is so flawed that when we wish to know who we are, the best approach would be to ask a friend who knows us well and who has a reputation for blunt accuracy. Not only is a sense of certainty infectious to our thinking, but it is also a perspective natural to our essence.

Craiutu, A. *Faces of Moderation: The Art of Balance in an Age of Extremes*, University of Pennsylvania Press, 2017. To sell a BCD, persuaders usually exaggerate to convince others. By stretching the truth, persuaders portray their ideas in the strongest fashion possible. This book is a masterful account of the necessity and perils of moderation throughout history. Increasing our understanding of the useful, habitual moderation of mind guards against dichotomous thinking, from which we speak of knowing "both" sides in a world where for most questions are a wide array of perspectives.

Damer, T. *Attacking Faulty Reasoning*, Wadsworth Publishing, 1987. While there are many compilations of logical fallacies, this one is outstanding for two reasons: First, despite the use of "attacking" in the title, a persistent theme in this book is the importance of keeping a conversation going. One of the negative conceptions associated with critical thinking is a sense that can be a weaponized pathway to dominating other people. However, Damer is highly sensitive to that potential and takes care to encouraging conversation derived from a desire to listen. A second strength of this book is the numerous colorful examples that tempt readers to keep reading.

Frazier, C. *Fear of Missing Out*, New Yorker, April 6, 2020. This humorous string of inevitable mistakes associated with even optimal decisions reminds us that the search for perfect decisions is a fool's mission. We can realistically work toward improved thinking, but perfect thinking as a goal is a polar bear safari in the Amazon River Basin.

Hardin, G, *Filters against Folly: How to Survive Despite Economists, Ecologists, and the Merely Eloquent*, Penguin Books, 1986. Like many outstanding books, this jewel makes us wonder "Why did I not write that?" Harden demonstrates that our thinking is damaged by high degrees of illiteracy, a reluctance to use numbers in our thinking, and a naivete about the simplicity of policy changes. The clarity and brevity of the book is a testament to Hardin's interdisciplinary virtuosity.

Huff, D. *How to Lie with Statistics*, W. W. Norton, 1993. Huff's book is a user-friendly volume for anyone who wants to go beyond the treatment of statistics as a source of information in our book. The illustrations and colorful stories used to describe the numerous abuses of statistics encourage those who fear numbers to endure the valuable lessons contained in this small book.

Ioannidis, J. P. A. *Why Most Published Research Findings Are False*, *PLOS Medicine*, August, 2005. If medical research contains many mistakes, it is probably a safe inference to think that other forms of information are similarly flawed. Professor Ioannidis is a hero for the important work he has done to urge care in releasing public health information. He has been a tireless critic of information prematurely announced as true.

Kahneman, D. *Thinking Fast and Slow*, Farrar, Straus, and Giroux, 2011. An important component of Friendly Critical Thinking ("FCT") is the essential role of humility in laying the foundation for FCT. Warrior critical thinking dehumanizes those who brutalize logic or the mandate for compelling evidence. Daniel Kahneman provides a narrative with evidence that warns readers that humans, regardless of their genetic gifts or educational accomplishments, struggle with a compulsive irrationality. That irrationality is as inescapable a limit to our decision-making skill as is the all too brief length of our lives.

Loftus, R. *Eyewitness Testimony*, Harvard University Press, 1996. Every year hundreds of people are convicted of a felony because jurors repeatedly exaggerate the factualness of eyewitness testimony. The research Loftus has contributed to debunking the dependability of eyewitness testimony is a strong antidote to the typical human perception error assuming that when a person remembers seeing something that perception is an unquestioned fact.

Mount, F. *Prime Movers*, Simon & Schuster, 2018. This book is a masterful reminder that even the most brilliant in our midst are burdened ultimately with their humanity with its inescapable bumbling and miscalculations. That Ghandi, Mary Wollstonecraft, Adam Smith, Karl Marx, and Thomas Jefferson provided us with incredibly stimulating analysis of human behave is unquestioned. However, those same thinkers were unable to transcend the frailties of being human. Each made mistakes of immense consequence. Critical thinking improves our thinking, but it lacks the capability to yield only wonderful perspectives. For instance, Ghandi lived a wise and inspirational life, but he was also very cruel to his children and spent almost no time in the village communities that he advocated for all of India.

Oreskes, N. *Is Science Actually 'Right'? Scientific American*, Vol. 325, No.1, July 20, 2021. Because we habitually assume that claims are true or false, biased or unbiased, or right or wrong, we regularly act as if we make decisions based on more and stronger knowledge than we possess. Humility should inform our thinking. However, because we do not understand how little we know, we speak and posture in a manner that ignores the distinction between probabilistic and universal truths.

Poisoned: The Dirty Truth about Your Food, 2023. This film makes a mockery of the repeated claim that the United States has the safest food in the entire world. It highlights how incredibly difficult it is for us to know about pathogens or microorganisms that cause disease from what we eat. If we are supposed to protect ourselves from disease passed from food producers to our collective gut, we require the assistance of regulators. Europeans, for instance, consume chicken with zero path; meanwhile, one out of four chickens sold in America is infected with salmonella.

Ruggeri, A. *The 'Sift" Strategy: A Four-step Method for Spotting Misinformation*, BBC, May, 5/12/2024 recovered at https://www.

bbc.com/future/article/20240509-the-sift-strategy-a-four-step-method-for-spotting-misinformation. This essay has a strong description of how to identify misinformation.

Sagan, C. *The Burden of Skepticism, The Skeptical Inquirer,* Vol. 12, No.1, July,1987. What is especially useful about this important essay is its highlighting of the tension between habitual skepticism and the necessity for openness to new ideas. The space between these two essential elements of critical thinking thrives only when we fight the inertia in obeying the dictates of either component of reflection.

www.ingramcontent.com/pod-product-compliance
Lightning Source LLC
Chambersburg PA
CBHW040934030426
42337CB00001B/8